Impossible Objects

BILL GREENWELL

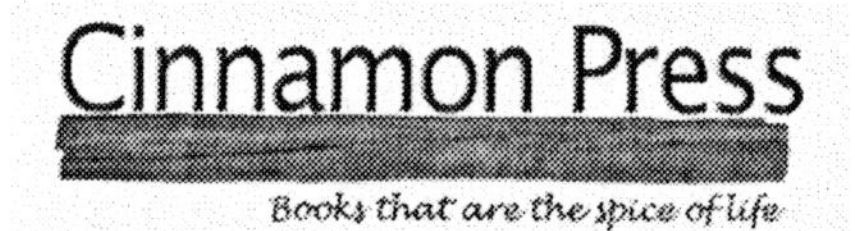

Published by Cinnamon Press
Meirion House
Glan yr afon
Tanygrisiau
Blaenau Ffestiniog
Gwynedd LL41 3SU
www.cinnamonpress.com

The right of Bill Greenwell to be identified as author of this work has been asserted by him in accordance with the Copyright, Designs and Patent Act, 1988. © 2006 Bill Greenwell - www.billgreenwell.com

ISBN 0-9549433-3-3
British Library Cataloguing in Publication Data. A CIP record for this book can be obtained from the British Library

All rights reserved. No part of this publication may be reproduced, stored in a retrieval system, or transmitted in any form or by any means, electronic, mechanical, photocopying, recording or otherwise without either the prior written permission of the publishers. This book may not be lent, hired out, resold or otherwise disposed of by way of trade in any form of binding or cover other than that in which it is published, without the prior consent of the publishers.

Designed and typeset in Palatino by Cinnamon Press
Cover design by Mike Fortune-Wood

Acknowledgements
I'd like to thank all of the following who've helped shape this collection: Lawrence Sail, Sandra Tappenden, Peter Sansom, Kate Carruthers, Peter Wilby, Sibylle Bonaert, Jan Fortune-Wood, Virginia Astley and Eithne Greenwell.

Some of the poems included here have been published previously in either printed or electronic format, in *Anon, Coffee House Poetry, The Flying Post, Iota, New Statesman, Odyssey, Orbis, Poetry Monthly, Smiths Knoll, Staple.* The author gratefully acknowledges the support of these publications and their editors.

Contents

for Gini, for Eithne

Praise for Impossible Objects:

Fresh, startling, inventive, entertaining… his enjoyment is infectious… Full of life, full of literary excitement and invention, these are the poems of a well stocked mind, allusive and witty. His images are sharp and arresting, but they're not forced or self-conscious… These are sideways poems, whose teasing perspectives are life enhancing. There's not a boring note here, not a hand-me-down idea. You never know where Greenwell's going next.

U A Fanthorpe & R V Bailey

Bill Greenwell does things with language you didn't know were possible… Fast and furious… like being a child… but he avoids being irritatingly self-congratulatory… – he's on a roll. Informed as he is by a lifetime's shrewd reading and adventurous…writing, Greenwell is utterly convincing… We trust him. And come to see he is doing more than having fun. Something darker is going on. Something only a skilled writer can deal with… Verbal pyrotechnics… so skilful, so celebratory and yet… there is this sinister subtext, a kind of dark passion that can't help appalling you as you read.

Selima Hill

I admire the precision of Bill Greenwell's language… his vocal range: recognizable but never a monotone… His passion and conviction; I smile… and belly laugh – at crazy jokes that turn serious or solemnity that turns hilarious. There's nothing trivial about his playfulness. These poems are much more than slick or smart; they are good.

Paul Hyland

Bill Greenwell's poetic landscape is both natural and surreal, observed and invented. A verbal magician working with the precision and economy of a master cartographer, he shows us dancing moons, teenage aphids, the East Pole… all manner of ordinary but extraordinary mysteries. The writing is witty and tender, delicate and tough. It consistently charms us out of the every-day… returns us with a refreshed and deepened sense of what that reality truly encompasses.

Carol Rumens

Impossible Objects

The Astronaut

I
As a Child

I spent my youth in practice,
kicking thin tin cans, or stringing

a line. My crackles were rationed:
they floated in sky-white milk

like lonely pod modules. I passed
behind the village pavilion,

pretending to be a golf-ball,
and tuning my wireless just to the

left of Hilversum. Golf-karts
crooned and zagged over crew-cut lawns,

and the meteors flew by my face
as I lay upwards in bunkers,

counting down the spasms of dusk.
Now my head is full of space.

II
Weeps

I look at the slow birth of Earth
through a portcullis of tears. My eyes

are raw: the reflections of starlight
dance on my visor. It is so hard,

harder even than thought to watch
a planet spin on faraway axes,

lost in night's spiral. I am waving
farewell. My heart is a fable,

an insoluble tale of grief.
It is written, in a thin tincture

of ink, or blood, and I write it,
marooned on a moon's soft blotch.

III
Dreams

Macramé of cable. My right eye
pulsing like a passing star.

The contraption I'm flying has wings,
but no controls at all. A blind

gulf in the window, and a U-turn
without a U, or a turn.

God's in the cockpit, repeating
Copy Copy in a coded voice

which reaches through thick ether
with something like gravity. Planets

pull at my pipes, there is rust
on the galley porthole, as I

teeter, looking for parachutes.
That's one small step ladder.

Gig

On bleed guitar, it's Johnny. He needs
no introduction (but he gets one. The audience
is crammed with amateur compères, each of whom
hopes for a booking
at the local library. They queue to roust
each other from their seats) and so:
On bleed guitar, it's Johnny. He plays
some shambled chords, assaults
A minor, and the gig –

But no. The drummer patrols his kit
like a traffic warden looking
for a lost ticket. He ups sticks, and slanders
a hi-hat. Johnny, in slash velvet, hits back, leaning
his lungs. He wraps his knuckles round the mike. Begins

a lyric. It fuses
everything he's ever learned, from being a cub
to drubbing his sister, from breaking the highway code
to
wolf hooey from the local woods
(where he rehearses, all teeth and tank-top,
in his private lair). The bassist
mumbles his thumbs, is several bars
ahead. He has been on medication. It might have been
meditation, in fact, but that's drugs for you. You

pop one, and your shadows
follow you round the stage. Johnny persists.
He plays for several hours, prowling and preening,
while the listeners peel off
and head for their bunk beds.

They lie there, brine, while lupine Johnny
thrashes the half-drawn dawn.

Missing Persons

They turn up, frayed at the edges,
yellowing, with lost images locked in their eyeballs,
and sanded shoes. If they have names
(and most of them don't) then these are
fictions hitched to their collars.

They are opened like wallets.
Out fall photos of mothers with milk-vetch eyes,
and ginger fingerprints, letters
written in Russian, wild hair
sealed in Sellotape, tired tickets
to nineteenth century shows. Stubs.

Someone runs a bath, and sponges
their wilting arms. A caucus of experts
tries them on adjectives, suffers them
to turn to
a lens, and, blinking, to give
what whittled looks they have left
to the music of platitude.

Later, they are left on benches, to grow
as old as they like. They stare at the blossom,
and the blossom dies. They are like empty parcels,
divested of string. Quartermasters
no longer call. One night, when no-one is looking,
they steal away, and become, somewhere, selves.

Recorded History

Face it. The borders are lined, are inked
with visible precision. This was the farmer's
leg of land, that hump the fold of stocking.

Sheep grazing on the map. Some shading
where they buried the cholera. That scratch
is where the sea sluiced the steeples.

I heard the scrawl of your throat, the way
it haggled the banns, how it sucked psalms
through a blackened snaggle of teeth.

Sat with the candle. The smoke withering
the air, shaping it. Outspread like damaged hands,
these scapes, these tatters. Isthmus,

peninsula, the straits across your forehead
as dangerous as a death. Tithes were paid
here, prompt as a dull sulk. Sign, scritch.

The trees here have been stripped of leaf,
and the barley brewed. Moss obscures the last
vestige of your illegible children.

The coast is unclear. Your crimped image
is stiff behind thick glass, under the balderdash
in the loft. I know you. And I know you not.

Domestic

I tossed a tantrum at you,
and it landed plum on your tongue.
The pin was still in.

You pulled it out like a conjuror
whipping a thorn from the paw
of his favourite rabbit.

Threw it. It stood in the air,
hanging above the open trap
like a super-cool blue balloon.

Hands unoccupied, we chucked
scraps of fabrication, and
knuckles of cold china.

The air was static. As were we.
And, waiting the tantrum's descent,
I knew that I'd catch it.

Tony Smoking Backwards

A Richard Billingham entry for the 2001 Turner Prize was the video,"Tony Smoking Backwards". Tony Blair was said at the time to be exhausted by war diplomacy.

I can't be fagged any more. My ashen
face is in this saucer, stubbling
the china, my packet's daily ration
exhausted. The fumes are troubling.

Here are the final embers, glowing
like a shortish fuse. They try to filter
the bad news. Now the smoke is flowing
out of my lungs, out of kilter

with my breath. It is running ragged
rings round my head: whenever I puff,
it sucks. It's soothing, since I'm haggard
extracting cancers. This stuff

kills? No? There's a war in my chest,
a hint of cough, bringing spit up.
The first drag of the dawn: it's best
to hawk. Time that I lit up.

Confection

He takes a handful of sweet
nothings, and wraps them in flash
wrappers. His jars are loaded
with invisible pastilles, promises.

Under his tongue, there is
a whistling comfit. He teases
his teeth with bits and baubles
of popular song.

When the child steps inside
his head, it makes a beeline
straight for the ribbons
of thought. Blueberry.

There is no mystique.
His hands are not cloven,
and the till still ringles
when the rainfall stalls.

Beer

I am in beer with you. The first time I saw you
I knew it was beer. Beer! said my father.
What do young men know
about beer? I would give beer
a wide berth, if I were you. What does

beer bring but weeping at night, and sickness
which curdles your words? This so-called beer,
it breaks the spirit, makes you
walk along sea-fronts, mumbling and foaming
This is it. This is beer. After a hard night
protesting beer, after a sleepless frenzy brought
on by beer, true beer you'd call it,
you haven't a leg to stand on.

But yes, beer all right. I want to make
beer with you, I want to write unpopular songs
about my beer, and sing them, because
I believe in beer at first sight, and that
true beer lasts forever. All the poets describe it,
even Larkin, who kept his beer secret,
but could not, under its influence, avoid the line
What will survive of us is beer.

The Sound of Rain on a Window

It's a sudden banter,
the arrival of several riddles at once,
nineteen people standing
in the road below, aiming
handfuls of pitted pebbles to see
if you're in.

They guess you're sleeping,
missed the bus, wrote
the rendezvous on the wrong calendar.

You wake
just as the sunlight hurries
back through the glass, asking
apologies, and painting
streaks where the rain
rattled your nerve. You stand

in the street, blinking,
throwing lonely stones
at your own window,
wondering whether you're in.

Moon

I
As a Child

The moon is a splinter of finger,
seen through a tear.

It is trapped in the night sky,
welded to dark.

It touches the cusp of nothing
and blinks, slowly,

while the whitened tide
covers the shingle's

tambourines, and blunders
up a green beach.

You found this moon weeping
one morning,

and carried it home.
This is your moon. This is

its cradle. This moon
has a beautiful future.

II
Two Moons

There are two moons,
revolving.

This moon's unsettled,
turning this way, that way
on its hesitant axis.

Its spindle hums
in the side of the night,
delirious as a discus
in flinted air.

This moon is settled
like a bedspread
under the smoothing of
patchwork hands.

Its quilt is like a feather
resting on the cusp
of a warm evening.

You find these moons
dancing the rhumba
on the corrugated surfaces
of blind tides.

Breathe in: let them
find a fulcrum.
They are still; they are new;
they will fuse. They are
sorting their orbit.

III
Glimpsed by Chance

The moon is a frosted pane,
through which the future
shifts like fragments of film:
shape and shimmy,
a fiasco of image. Scrimshaw.

You carve your initials
into its bright white wood, and it
bleeds like a cherry,
a diary, a memory you pressed
between pale paper.

It is canny, uncanny,
a moon full of promises,
pools, something tussling your hair
when breezes
are blown along by songs.

You find this moon
when you open your hand
in your sleep.
It rests on your fingers.

Enclosures

I stand in a hiatus of field,
looking over the hedges, rumpled
by shadow, staring
at the skimp of the horizon's line.

You're beside me. The sea
is over the hill, listening
to how well-defined our conversation is,
while we inspect these half-

fallen walls. It isn't clear
how long this gate's been crippled,
nor when it knuckled
under pressure of time.

*

The mat is crammed with letters,
brown and white, filled
with your messages. They contain
a mixture of the meagre

and the replete, and I spill
the contents across the stained table
where today I am weeping
blue-grey tears. I shuffle

them into disorder, open them.
Some of your sentences
don't start. Others are full
of chintz, of no constraint.

*

The fringes of the field are cut
by blunt scissors. Here fences
are fixed; here wooden poles
patrol the perimeters.

There are job lots of oblong,
crazy palings with their wire
strung out. In a shawl of shade,
we open the rucksack,

and pull out the picnic,
talking about trees. And see
how they too order the land,
strip it of innocence.

*

Our conversations cover
the table, a stenographer's
record of what we said,
your steady hand transcribing

the best bits. Some letters
breeze open, like larks.
This silence transfixes me,
slams my lips quite shut.

Lots to say, you say, *but*
don't know what's appropriate.
Nor do I. And so I store
your letters, neat, in a drawer.

*

Streams and ditches mark
the map of the fields. Streams
meddle the edges, make them
tease the eye. Each ditch

bevels the earth, and furrows
the view. I turn to you.
You aren't enclosed at all;
I feel like breaking open

my caution, letting it breathe.
But I don't. I let the birds
flutter inside me like clocks
shocked by new pendulums.

The Stories of Your Lives

Life One

This was some story.
You threw your weight
at a guitarist who strangled his chords,
and who went off
with a dancer who doubled the huff.

Bored, you made
fruit pies, and lived off the crusts
of your customers.

One Sunday, you were orphaned,
and fell from a pedestal
into a fountain, and drowned.

Life Two

This was a tell-tale.
You grew up in an attic, with toy-chests,
and a rockabilly horse.

Your mother was really your mother,
but you thought
she was your maiden aunt.

At seventeen, you eloped with a viola
to see the world.
You found Norfolk,

and lived in a flat with a man
who worshipped the sea,
who ate pilchards from the tin.

One night you died laughing
after an argument over his bloaters.
You couldn't make it up.

Life Three

This was just matter-of-fact.
You lived in a tree-
house, with curtains and carpets,
and a feral cat.

You fell in love with a body-builder
(he used a kit)
and polished his muscles.

One day the cat got his tongue.
Depressed, you moved trees.
It was through grief that you met
the life-saver
who couldn't swim to
save his life. He
died in your arm-bands.

Since then you have drawn water
in a sketch-book.
No-one knows to what end.

Life Four

They still talk about this one.
You were raised in a trance,
until, without ado,
you kissed a superstitious vicar
in a chancel.

But he was already married
(by himself) to a wife
with fifteen infants and a smack habit.

Some say
you were wasted away.

Absent Fathers

Absent fathers stand in parks,
cupping their smokes like cuckoo-spit
and watching the swings fly high.

Their eyes lie flat against their heads,
taking evasive inaction.

In winter, when the children go,
and roundabouts are frozen sick,
they clap themselves mechanically
and study their watches.

When they missed the rehearsal,
they found themselves without a line
or even a squint of the limelight:

they are walk-ons, extras.
In their chafed faces, you can still see
the silhouettes of intention,

before the absence, and before
the daily pilgrimage to the child's slide.

Impossible Objects

The East Pole. A happy-go-lackey.
The grimace of sphinxes.
A mink in a mink coat. Tobacco
Crescent. Someone who thinks his

boots are in his heart. A comet
with a wet tail and a cold nose.
Residence in a poet. Wallace and Grizelda.
Someone who chose

not wisely but two wells, and a bucket
without a handle. Tuppence-
threepenny. A whale in Nantucket
on its summer holiday. Weapons

of mass disarmament. Keeping
your temper when someone is shoving you
in the back. The sound of stars weeping.
Finding a hornet's pulse. Not loving you.

Gun Lore

I'm loaded, well-oiled. The spick
slug of myself may well protrude
in a manner considered crude.

I'm smooth, on the verge of slick;
there's more of this in my pocket
which means business. I've a dual

purpose: if you fill me with fuel,
my eyes light up. Don't knock it.
There's some who'd call this filthy,

scheming. I'm loaded, big shot
holding sway in crowded bars, hot
and sticky and very stealthy,

like an eye. I'm both barrels
loaded. It's a potent feeling,
to roam your territory, wheeling

and firing. I have no quarrels.
So what? I am at the ready,
greased, with a calculated snub:

better face it, fast. The nub
of me's rapid response. Steady.
I'm dangerous whenever goaded

because I'm full of it. Place
your hand on my bulging case.
Stand back. Let me through. I'm loaded.

Tournesol

The sunflower does not turn to the sun. T. Moore (1814) says 'The sunflower turns on her god when he sets'... This may do in poetry, but it is not correct.

– Dr. Brewer's Reader's Handbook (1911)

I stare the sun's hard eyeball out,
until blind, like a bunion.
The widow rings her baltic bell,
and sea freezes. She hauls

her heart behind her, and curls,
hook-backed, against the frosted
and salty waves. Bathers, oiled
like pink pilchards, raise fists

and other blunted instruments. There's
never a lifeguard when you
want to rescue your tan. I'm out
in a tirade of rain, taking the air

out of bottles, which are fashioned
from sand, soda and lime.
That's how they stick together,
as limpets do. The widow turns

in her sea-weeds, counting hours
and polishing the old glaze
of crackled tide. On the beach,
the trippers hide behind their pyjama

windbreaks, and play *tournesol*
with boiled bodies. My job
is planting black flags along the front,
which isn't a picnic, frankly.

The world's on a swivel, all of it,
searching for grief and what
that means. Which may do in poetry,
although of course, it isn't correct.

Crumbs

Your bed was filled with crumbs,
and occasional stains
of lime marmalade, of mornings
when we woke, unwrapped,
hearing the early cough of the cars.

We stank of sleep. The sheets
were still faint, damp
where we'd come at each other
like cutlasses. Nights were mayhem:

we brawled all through them,
clinching each other. We had secret
repertoires of skin, and we played
all the tunes at slow tilt.
You spilt the tea, climbing through
half-light, back to the bed, carrying
more toast, more marmalade, more crumbs.

All mist, no sea

Your early walk, tentative,
each footstep a tipple. You're wearing
silent plimsolls. They cross the
rasp of the road, as quiet as thieves.
The raw grass at your ankles.
Breathless. Your diary writes itself
like moss on stone. You open
the curtains on three fathoms of sea, and hear
whistling at the window, like pencil
fooling on paper.

Some stars, if you like.

Out here, you smooth your hands,
and warm them in mist.
You take three wisps and plait them
unconsciously, your hair
frizzing in instants.
There is sand between your toes. You stoop
to brush it away, like a duchess
who has mislaid her maid. You cannot
read your writing;
the ebb rinses its meanings, touches
your face.

Half-Century Dads

for Rose

Hands up, whose Dad is in his twenties?
A couple of pale, uncompromising arms,
the fingers wibbling. The teacher, weirdly
beardless, consults himself. They're ten, and therefore –
note down, social, problem, at risk. Tsk.

Hands up, whose Dad is in his thirties?
Up go the antlers. Like looking across an estate
palpitating with aerials. Calculate percentages:
the next homework, perhaps. The teacher
thinks smoothly of the wife he's not acquired.

Hands up, whose Dad is in his forties?
A fair few, few but fair enough. They waited
for the bones to settle, until they'd saved
the strength of their convictions. Then, on the
bounce, three. Twins and another. He grins.

Hands up, whose Dad is in his fifties?
The chairs give a narrow squeak, like
polystyrene. Three shifty kids pop up their palms,
and shut their eyelids. The teacher's raucous
inside. One of the three dribbles a dead tear.

Hands up, whose Dad is in his sixties?
At the side, in the shadow of the broken blackboard,
something shivers. The bunched hand is fragile.
The teacher sees it stroking a casket. Sad,
really. To have a father who knew the wireless.

Hands up (this is a joke) whose Dad is in
his seventies? Better. The children's eyes
skiffle the room. The teacher turns to his list,
ticks it quick. Numeracy hour. He misses
the other one, plum tomato cheeks, hands up.

Troubadours

They used to show up, nattily,
at the lips of windows, plunking their way
through tortuous tearjerkers.
Seventeen verses through dawn's hot flush,
the birds nodding their feathery heads
or just tapping their beaks on the branches,
they'd sign off with theme tunes,
a strum, a modal yodel,
and some mucky proposal or other.

Packs of them cramming corners
before streets had even been built for them,
fingernail-pickers, strutting their fret-boards
and their Blondel good looks
just underneath your casements:
ooby-dooby troubadours, chancing their
arms and their puff sleeves with silvery
serenades, refrains, and encores.
Woo, woo. Hey.

Woh.

Now I send you slim cassettes,
tucked into jiffy bags, wrapped in
anonymity, mail-order melodies so that
your husband shan't suspect.
You have me taped. I lift my lyrics,
my shivering guitars from the long racks
of lovers available. I do not
stand by your dustbin, bruising lungs,
busting a catgut to snatch your attention.

And I pay my ventriloquists plenty,
cash words in their mouths, let love
loose through your earphones. Woo
yeah. Woh. I am your
troubadour. I am in
stereo, too.

Keeping Fit with Jesse James

Each afternoon he exercised... he scraped his sweat off with a butter knife - Ron Hansen

In corpore sano.
Rides himself bareback,
lets his body bathe in sweat,
soaks himself up like applause, stands,
bends horseshoes straight with his hands.

Bruises his palms
as the flashing axe pulps the good wood.
Under the sunlight, suspenders down,
whirls two yellow pins
in a blur of arcs, and begins

to glister. Holsters
hang low. Muscles pumping,
jumps the surrey up from a squat
nineteen times, preens. Out of doors
the butter melts, golden, from his pores.

Dunks his fresh head
in the horse's bucket. His son,
six, is hunched on his honeyed shoulders.
Toes snag the garter snakes
gently. Whatever it takes.

How to kill yourself

With kindness. This is the hardest.
You need to sling a smile
round your neck, and
give yourself a bit of a break.

With a gin sling. This
is a lethal cocktail, and when the world
swirls before your eyes,
you need to make several
before you're ineffective.

With a bitter pill. The doctor
will make you swallow
hard, and may recommend
that you seek a second
opinion. So that takes time
and a deal of trouble.

With a smashed heart.
Usually works. Just fall in love
with someone who cannot
love you, and vice versa.
The heart, mind you,
is a muscle. Ask your
butcher to prepare you.

Or stop breathing. It helps
if you ask someone else
to hold your breath, gently.

Cleansing Fluids

for Sarah Hopkins

CTC: my mother kept it
at the back of a larder, in a snap-shut dark-green
Gordon's gin-bottle, on the top shelf
with spiders. It was a problem solvent.
It removed stains from shorts and skirts,
from souls. It could lift gum, grease,
flies, lies. It was tick-toxic. It was sweet.
I wondered
how my father could drink the stuff.

TCP: we can only graze
the surface of this subject. It is the skeptic
of antiseptics. It can do knees, shins, sins,
and also drains. Worrying, that. That you can
purge guilt with something which cleanses
everything, including the kitchen sink.
It disinfects the self.
Search for it on gargle.

DDT: it beats the mosquito, the louse, the Colorado
Beetle, and Cary Grant if you close-shave
an Indiana scrub. It craps the crops.
It stops the heart from hurting, and cleans up
weevil and evil. We used to eat it
in stews, in sandwiches, and in confessionals
which steamed like saunas.
It was mammon from heaven. They banned it
like Bibles in affirmation class.

PLC: This took the business out of family
like jam from a dead doughnut. It takes the heat
out of cleaning up, and it cleans up quickly, too.

TLC: This is the one I meant. It softens
the ducts, pardons the peccadillo, and hugs
one another in pale pink towels. Angels
recommend it. It wipes away stains on the cheeks
and washes the wicked feet. It is best
in a bath. It beats its wings like feather-breath
and tastes like a month of sundaes.

Teenage Aphids

Many aphids are born pregnant.

Oh yeah, that is like so gay.
I mean, like I was born pregnant,
okay, I mean
so what.

So what
is a carcass? It is my mummy? Are you
kidding me?

Take a leaf
out of your own garden. Like I wouldn't
eat my greens, your greens,
would be a starving larva? Are you a
damsel bug, a pirate, give you a bag of thrips?
No way. Give me some juice
for some honeydew.

Okay, my appetite. So it's sugar, sugar.
I eat my own weight in babies.
I take after my mum, like she is so me.
I am millions, sky high, I can move
more miles than you can shake my schtick at.
What?

Don't give me that so ladybird
routine. Oh okay. Plenty more
where I came from.

The Swizz

In my day, we had the swizz.
Most things could be pinned on it,
an absence of Mintoes, the rota
for washing the dog being altered,
the price of a packet of lies
(which was bed, bath, a ban
on *Bonanza* and straight to your
room, if they got the order wrong).
Each of these was a swizz.

You could practise its ignoble art,
swapping a cracked marble, say,
for a set of false conkers,
but swizzes were essentially
against you, a mild violence
crumpling the equanimity
of a cheerful and peaceable childhood.

The swizz is extinct. Official.
It went the way of Spangles,
Cremola Foam, the interlude,
the trolley bus, a third of a
pint of milk at playtime,
and the threepenny bit.

In came lager, the avocado,
pots of yoghurt, the salt
and vinegar crisp, satellites,
and regular invitations
to enter a pension scheme.

What a swizz.

Genius

He was a bright spark, said the professionals,
testing him on his embers and the tank
regiments which patrolled his pituitary gland.
Night-times, he'd read Meccano by starlight,
under invisible sheets. He locked his collars
with a plumstone stud. Cook helped him
when he invented the mulchless bucket.
He patented a style of patent, with his left hand.

The doctors had said to beware dimwits.
When his uncle threw him, like a discus,
into the gelid sea, he shrugged his long lungs
and took up the scuba position. Dived
through the snout of a wave. Swallowed a minnow,
whose snazzy skin lay coolly under his breath.
They retched when he brought back an atlas
open on a page of hitherto unknown ocean.

Sex he took with a pinch of snuff. His girl
was a velveteen bodice. She lay all day tangled
in the barb of his body, and married him suddenly.
The banns were still warm. They cultivated
the villagers, and taught them the arts of lawning,
rigging, and prayer. He abandoned his parents
on a tabloid doorstep with pyjamas, and a note:
These people taught me nothing that I knew.

His obituaries were flecked with dead spittle.
They spoke coldly of the precipice, of the skeeter
of his fingernails on the thinning air, the lamps
unlit in his scalded eyes. He was dissembled.
His widow took root in an attic of feral cats.
She was the last to speak his language, and wired
her jaws. Biographers could not shift his story,
and collapsed into platitude. No-one succeeded.

Ancient History

The plan to defeat Iraq in a week was described by ITV's Mark Austin as "ancient history".

This is the land of algebra:
where Genghis Khan and Tamburlaine
dipped their vicious toes
in the rivers' abstractions, with authority
above simple numbers.

The pill-box, the kill-box, the hanging
gardens of Babylon,
the suburbs of murder. Moving fingers
and desiccated limbs: it's a short
step from Nebuchadnezzar
to Chemical Ali.

Sunlight is stunning, and absorbs
the *x* and *y* of the missiles.
A general says "I have a lot of tools
in my toolbox"; as witness
his blunt, adulterated instruments.

Just look how the land lies,
how flexible equations can be, how
effects-based the severed head.
How smart the vertical
envelopment. Add up the tomatoes
in the Assyrian bazaar. Here is
the algebra of ancient history,
in the land which dreamed up zero.

Tumbledown House

This house has seen better days.
Its great quiff of thatch
has quite collapsed, and the straw
stiffens like the giant wings
of old-age ravens left out in rain.

There may be voices
simmering inside, asking where
light is, and what sanctuary there is
in dust's demesne. Their prayers
are muffled, obscure,
mumbo-mouthed, breathless like
hinges in a rain-drenched door.

We sit in the chapel,
snacking on apples. Here the air
is as cool as bloom.
We have started to unpick
each other's riddles, and to open
the hymnals of our lives.

In the tumbledown house,
the window, a parallelogram,
looks out in witness as we walk our way
past it. We lob the cores
over a sun-deckled hedge, you first.
Our voices are chiming.
If I looked for a rhyme, I would find it
in your face, in mine, in the moment
you grazed your fingers
over my arm.

The tumbledown house is charmed;
birds rise in flight
from its hesperus chimney
and waken the neighbours
with silver canticles.

New Geography

A hundred times I have asked myself whether it is possible
that the world's geography is incomplete
- Willis George Emerson, *The Smoky God*, 1908

The single helix
of this hill: like a narwhal's
left tooth. I climb its white corn
and measure
the world in widdershins.

Fog underwater
confuses the shoal's sonar.
They mass around me,
gelatinous,
think I'm a shipwreck.

A salty river
shivers with friction. Its tides
shift aimlessly along these frosted banks,
like brides
banned from a clambake.

The upside tree
roots in the costive air, haggling.
I burrow under the trunk,
and stuff
my teeth with its earthen fruit.

Coincidences

There's a light on somewhere. There's a light
on somewhere else. There's a light
breeze blowing. Coincidence. That both
cabins should be occupied by a barbershop
quartet called Close Shave.

On the strop of nine, a man called Man
walks over the grave
of a chandler called Wick. Coincidence.
That they were both at school
in Bury, in 1976. It was a hot summer.

The sun beats its tantrum on the lid
of a corrugated cow-shed. It is filled
with sheep. Coincidence. Last week, I ate
a chump chop and some sirloin steak.
Mixed grill. No sausages.

An old banger turns up at a garage,
and explodes with laughter. The smoke
clears. Coincidence. The mechanic
is wearing a bonnet, and I'm wearing
a hood. Which one is American?

Two planes fire 500 shells
at a Middle East seaside. The road's
red. Coincidence. They're not
writing poems in the sky,
and neither am I.

Take It Away

Witnesses heard her,
the throe over, after the cuts,
and the child skidding its lips
on the nipple.

"Take it away," she said.
Her eyes were ditch. They shambled
over the bloodied body,
slicing the fresh air dead.

"Take it away," she told them.
They scratched it in their memories,
storing the caustic, shutting
their ears to the echo.

No-one heard (and she'd never remember)
that moment when they stuffed
the new child on her breast,
how, hearing the blur, the absurd
image of Joe Loss occurred to her:

his baton poised, the band at a standstill.
She heard him move, tap
the ticking stick at the drummer.
He moved like a smirk. And then,
seeing the baby stuck to her breast,
he nodded the band into frantic action.

"Take it away," she said, beaming.

On the Resolution, 1772-1775

I will not say it was impossible any where to get farther to the South; but the attempting of it would have been a dangerous and rash enterprise. - James Cook, 1774

I.

Whey of faces, the milk light
pastes the crew like spooks:
hulks of ice drift at leisure
through cracking latitudes.

Some outrigger bergs bombard
the oceans with ragged slabs:
noise shivers the nerves like bone,
crenellates the waves.

In the chylous sea, the captain
tracks the mists, far past
wallowing bobs of obstacle,
blubber and the petrels' echo.

The landscape is tantalus, rocks
anchored in sheer agonies,
a weld of crags, cramped bang
on the world's underbelly.

II

Fog dogs us, and we must beat
tyrannies of sleet.
Squalls will capsize us. Our wake
freezes behind the vessel.

Incognita, australis: we
orbit the peripheries,
awkward as we tack our route
along a coast of clefts.

The aurora pulses and we guess
at the depth beneath, strain
our lost eyes for energy. The lodes
are silver beneath the pack.

Desperadoes

There was a scorch of feathers,
and the vulture pulled up, panting,
at the edge of town.
Hick hat, the spark of spurs,
drunks up-ended in the water-trough.
Even the air was creaking.

I tethered the vulture to the sheriff,
packing his punches flat, like banknotes.
His trigger finger had shingles:
the sun had unpeeled
the price on my head. It was pleasant
to feel properly wanted.

I made a buntline for the hooch
stashed in the old saloon.
They were passing stetsons, forgetful,
and drinking their linseed quickly,
dealing out desperate hands.
Some of their tongues had stubble:

their eyelids were made of lead.
The floorboards were parched. I took
the skid from a bottle,
biting the liquor's bullet. They'd heard
rumours about my alias.
My eyes were as dry as a gulch.

By sun-up, we sprawled
like shadows across the clapboard.
We had drunk both barrels,
lay face up in the dust,
waiting to ambush
the posse of camera crews.

Unmarked

You fell out of the unmarked album
where someone had tucked you
with thin thumbs.

A poor likeness, perhaps. Your elbow
rests, vaguely, on a rough wall.
Perhaps it isn't you at all:

disengaged, undated, your half-head
garnished with no hat,
you start with stark eyes, and a trim

smile, and stop at your ankles.
The photographer cut you
out of context, distracted, no doubt

by your cranky collar, no tie,
the heat of what might have been
a moment. Even your trousers,

uncreased, are anonymous. Sun
stains the spare air to your right.
And here you aren't,

stuck in a slab of album
at the back of the poorly drawer
where someone once kept you.

The Golden Fleece

I collect them, see. Wind-
cheaters, filled with warmth and Gortex,
cagoules, the pink tops
of shell suits discarded at auctions
by bidders, Barbours
thrown over a mahogany gate
with Acid Drops in their pockets,
and parkas (Swedish Army M90 with hood in
particular). Combat jackets,
with and without winter
camouflage. Banff ones, and every
conceivable fleece. Bombers and quilts,
the pakamac, freestyle down vests
with heavy duty zippers, and
welded seams. All these I collect,
catalogue numbers and all,
being an anorak.

You open the door

and the cat comes in, humming, from next door.
Behind your back. Well that's all right, but
in his mouth he carries
a can of worms, which you open
and in it, you find a bottle, corked,
with a message in it,
from an old salt, and in the message
you read words. And in the words
are
the sounds of waves, prowling the prow
like mutineers, and in the waves
you hear the hands of God
rinsing the world of bloodstains, pain, the pandemonium
of martyrs, the spittle of innocents,
and the boiled anger of man.

Look what the cat's brought in, you say,
showing it to the door.

White Jigsaw

in memory of Clare

You come here with a jigsaw
the colour of clouds,
tranquil, like milk in alcohol,
but filled with the brilliant
white of sunlight.

You're going to let me down
and leave me flat.

The mist at Bamburgh's lifting:
across the long sands
the tide is riffling a tune.
Three buckets and spades,
waiting. Maud, Lily and Kate.
Drop that and get on deck.
You're wearing a ring
in the daft shape of a duck.

Meticulous, tetchy,
your fingers are filled with string, you've
been
shopping for Christmas
the year after the year
after next.

Wake up, I've got something
to say to you. Stay with me.
You're everywhere and nowhere baby,
that's where you're at.

We play *The Birthday Cakewalk*
by Russ Conway, at 78 r.p.m.
and race round the chesterfield
laughing like loons.

Our boat nudges through weed
in the jungle shade. Our faces
are streaked with mud. We screech

at the leeches, the leeches.
Both of us are nominated
for Oscars.

Throw the dice, and move
the boat, the dog, the ship:
Monopoly, Totopoly,
Tri-tactics. The games
will persist, days, weeks,
months and years.

You laugh like a drain,
and clap your hand to your head
like a pirate.

I've got something to say
that'll cause you pain.

Guess what, you ask.
I'll be losing my eye,
I'm pregnant. I've landed
on Mayfair.

You're like our grandmother,
lying there serene, on
the white bed in Bart's.
There is a twinkle
in your eye
the size of a laugh.

Clare, the last thing you said
to me was
Night Night Daddy.

There is a Dégas ballerina
dancing above your bed.
The jigsaw sits on the table,
neat and tidy,
as with consummate skill
you fill each space,
your fingers finicking
the spindrift of white
into a wild, inviolate sky.

A glass of wine. Here.
You can't do that. The light
is intense, it is linen,
it is antarctic, it is
razzle-dazzling. I
love you. Here it is, Clare, it is
the last, impossible piece.

Openers

M. Paul Valéry recently suggested that an anthology be compiled in which the largest possible number of opening passages from novels be offered; the resulting insanity, he predicted, would be a source of considerable edification.

(André Breton – Surrealist Manifesto, 1924)

There was no possibility of taking a walk that day
because someone else had
taken it earlier. When they returned, before breakfast,
ready for kedgeree, they told the concierge
that the walk was at the bottom of a weir,
having run away – enthusiastically – with half an idea.

Ours is essentially a tragic age, so we
refuse to take it tragically. We laugh under sufferance,
under the bright red blanket which the nurse
uses to protect us from photographers, as she leads us
into the ambulance. Dying is so strange.
It hurts like calculus, and you never get over it.

All happy families are alike. Mr. Bun the Baker, Mrs. Bun
the Succubus, Master Bun the runaway sensation,
Miss Bun the disco diva, Uncle Bun the close friend
of Mrs. Bun, Bun the cat, the other Miss Bun, Mavis, who
is no relation, and lours the hours away cleaning ovens
and getting into hot water to beat the bathroom queue.

This is the saddest story I have ever heard. Two smiles
collide in mid-air, and turn to a kiss.
They raise cattle, and Cain, and the spirits of those
who rustle net curtains like veils. They dig wells
as if there were no today. They mother each other,
and are left in a rest home, under a fond illusion.

If you really want to hear about it, why bother
with pain? You wake with wilting eyes, with white ash
dusting your thighs, strapped to a stretcher,
while an artist covers your canvas with oranges, apples,
a vase. Still life. Being in love is bayonet practice.
You want to surrender, but alas, you have no arms.

Attics

You go down to the attic,
hefting your epaulettes, looking for salvage.
Hoping for trove. Down in the loft
there is a fat chance of falling
over feet
and inches of dry dust. You turn up
your used uniforms, the blest years of your life.

Mouldering, in the depths
of your attic's despair, you find your second
best bed-socks, your first will and testament.
You have left everything
to yourself. Even your medals.
The pedal-cycle from which you fell
at Gallipoli. The green jeans
which your aunt ironed one weeping afternoon
when you lay in the hollyhocks
and plunged your cutlass into next door's cat.

Here is the ear-trumpet
through which you blew round raspberries
at the corporal. Here is the ghost of your chance.
Here, underground, is the chalk,
the stick you used to count the hours
when your cousins slammed you in jankers.

The things you didn't do. Certificates
of children you never had. Wastes of time.
Anthologies of dogs and cats.
Castanets. The strips you tore from non-commissioned
officers, in your holiday heyday.
In this catacomb, the bulbs blown
into cold bloom, you find what you weren't
looking for. Your feet.

The Invisible Man in Love

I shrug my dumb shoulders,
my see-through heart bobbing
on radio waves.

The ghost of a smirk
lurks on the ledge of my lips.

Or I pine, a shadow
of a shadow of myself,
like breath on a temperate day
or a portrait of taste.

I am in love with a nurse.
I study her shoes, their clop,
the white linen boat which crests
the wave of her hair,
and the broken watch which she wears,
her medal, on her chest.

In heat, I am practically
gelatinous, almost a mirage,
a haze of desire.

Now I am randy for bandage.
I wrap raw gauze round my ankles,
my feet, and soon I am
a rough pair of puttees.

The cotton is hot. I ravel
my thighs, my hips, my belly
in swathes of importunate shape.
Cummerbund, napkin, webbing, chinstrap.
I slice lines for mouth, eyes, ears.

My skull bulges.
Now I am mannequin,
now I am man. This is
an emergency.

I hide in the hospital store
with the swabs and prosthetics.
Hearing the pedantry of her heels,
her beddable voice, I tremble.

And think of her frank hands
undressing me.

Pass Notes

When I was a boy,
they waltzed me into the wall
of examinations. I was served

a worm of string,
and a slab of paranoid paper.
Women in ginger slippers

patrolled the hall,
skating the iron silence
with wide eyes in the sides

of wizened heads.
I huddled my limbs, and waited
for bells to ring which didn't:

instead, I poised my
special pen, steady and deaf
until they tidied my name away,

and turned me out.
I've led a fugitive existence, since:
no good, it seems, at being good.

To help my child,
I have made the front room a replica
of all examination halls.

To quell his nerves,
meals are invigilated. I watch
(as does my wife) the spoons pass

the test of his lip.
He has memorised the membrane
of every pea upon his plate.

Everything

She remembered everything, suddenly, lying in bed
and catching farthings of light in one cupped hand.
It came out of nowhere, like fear. The way she'd paused,
out walking, to ask where she was. How she'd coaxed
words from an unwilling throat, wrapped them in speech,
and driven them to the station. It was (she'd confessed)
just a matter of misunderstanding: whitewash sky,
the peal of inclement bells, her caulked mouth, drizzle,
trees cuckolded by leaves, the jealousy of birdsong.

It was everything, a surrender of sorts, she thought,
reaching for tea. At every footfall, she had been visiting
memorials and haunts and the spent mnemonics
of love affairs, the beaten tattoos of emptied sentences,
the way that pink mimosa resembles feathers, the skylarks
in her thighs, the judder of lust, the craven humps
of earth in the graveyard. Her mouth tasted of moss.
She came to a wall, walked through it. This was where
dawn once spilt itself over her, filled her with elegy.

She drew her sheets around her, bandaging everything,
huddling herself, half-angry that it had all just tumbled
over her, without warning or warmth. Her eyes
were wine-stained, all her death and birth and love
and song and pain came in concentrated waves
which washed her body, gulped her up. Over fields
of savage wheat and breeding barley, she was tracing
which way she'd walked. Oh she had survived, she flew
round her life, and held herself tight, in spite of everything.

The Need to Panic

I have known the shooting of a star spoil a night's rest, and have seen a man in love grow pale and lose his appetite upon the plucking of a merrythought... There is nothing so inconsiderable which may not appear dreadful to an imagination that is filled with omens and prognostics. A rusty nail or a crooked pin shoot up into prodigies.

-Addison (The Spectator, No. 7, March 8th, 1710-11)

The plane tree flakes; when old, it swells
as if its neck were clogged up with conundrum.
Your gorge rises. The world leans
on the lobe of your shoulder. The leaf-hair
makes you scream with asthma.

Maidenhair looks like ice-green crystals;
it stinks like a dangerous lily. You
are fraught with spores. Sleep heaps
your skin with startled sweats.
You wake, grained with dangerous laughter.

A dragonfly hauls itself from water,
which it has haunted. It whirrs, furious.
Somebody's died. You run the room
like a rat on a catafalque, and break
every pain in your body.

The third-hand car swerves, googly,
into a dry-stone wall. The engine ticks
like an unfit flea. You hear burning
but that's just the way that the rust
settles. *Oh Christ the way the window opens*

Here's a merrythought to snap your heart.
You slept like a drum. You took the day
off the hook, and copped off with a cloud.
That's love lodged underneath your ledge,
and it shoots you, like a star-burst.

A merrythought is a wishbone.

RPM

At 16, there's little revolution, no
spin to speak of, it's kids' stuff.
Most of it is all talk.

Tubby the Tuba is led gently,
extensively to bed, and Danny Kaye
is a nervous night nurse.

At 33, everything is much clearer.
You may turn slowly but decisively
feeling the needle describe its circle;
there is time to register that sigh
as the stylus lifts; you may play
both sides, too, if you turn over.

You can choose where to start,
there are options. It will probably
take you, what, forty-plus minutes
to do it real justice, and you'll have
invested so much more.

At 45, the shebang is quicker.
Three minutes, however you practise,
and the flipside's forgettable.
You scratch easily, and you warp
when the weather's warm.

You are restricted to seven inches.

At 78, you are so quick
you miss it, and the arm
shoots to its rest. You can't
hear the words for crackle, you are
brittle as water biscuit.
You fracture too frequently.
You'd be better off with a wind-up.
It makes you feel dizzy, no-one
takes you seriously, you're mainly
remaindered, there are loads of you
in charity shops.

On Style

I write you rambling letters
on foolscap, quarto, loops and skirls,
the punctuation thudding
like hammers on a knackered upright.

You write me post-its,
tickertape, ribbons of ink
tied to photographs of cloud formation.

I compose soliloquies
and sign them like testaments,
balancing paragraphs and folding
word over word over word.

You dance from line to
line, erotic spirals, catchy
tunes you lose on the way to the post-box.

I fill the wide open fields
with trestle tables, and imagine
a thousand invisible clerks
taking the gist of my dictation.

You empty an inkpot
over a passer-by.

I bury subtexts between
salutation and valediction,
gravely nodding over the grammar
and cursing the hands on the clock.

You send me
distractions, lullabies.

I monitor dates, record
their tiny indentations on paper
like a night-watchman counting
thousands of different minutes.

And you give me love
on the white
wing of an envelope.

You walking

the gauntlet of beech trees
(it is wet underfoot)
while a spiv sky
          whistles above you

walking the treacherous route, the one
sketched in on the
map by a stranger (with
a cockle hat, and
          a loose tooth). You walking

on fire, the sparks dinking
in the half-dark, your feet
pulping the earth
and your ankles bruised
          like dull blush, you

walking. Milestones. The level
energy of thought propels you
towards the clinker
of lumpety unmade roads,
          where walking you

push the breath through lips
caulked by the mist,
and follow the algebra
of dawn towards logical
          conclusions, spinning

inside like a gyroscope,
your molten face
tipsy within, as if tasting
sloes, turning them
          into gin on

your lip, hands jammed in pockets,
your eyelids
flustered with sunlight
to come, and you
          walking from here

to there, slip-happy to
be composing yourself
for something
underneath the whimsy of sky where there's
you
          walking.

The Muse

I
Wanted Posters

She keeps a stash of them,
under her ironing. Some of their inks
have made faint veronicas
on her linen. Their faces

cannot be traced, cannot be found
in files, their cases have closed
like souvenir seasides in winter.
Their eyelids are shuttered.

She found them nailed to trees,
or pasted on lost windows, offering
outrageous rewards. And all she needed
was to roust out a rondel,

come up crackers and trumps
with a simple glimmer,
wrap it in ribbon and let the
skies have it, an improbable kite.

Instead, the poet, all stubble
and empty headlines, lies blithely
between the cream-white leaves
of forgotten washing.

II
Something Better to Do

Excuse me, do I look as if
I've been lounging around at the Parthenon?

The muse removes her sling-backs,
polishes her shades,
swallows her coffee like cyanide,
and eats air.

Yes, there were nine. Their names
are chiselled into the mountains.
They were as thirsty as thieves. They needed
milk (full
cream), water and the
buzz of best honey.

The muse watches the sunshine
botching the shadows. She hums.
She has a voice like softened coriander.

No idea. They remembered
memories in the days before
the database. They wore dresses
of alabaster, and took the sea air
into their early morning mouths.
Their kisses were moths. They had never
seen an ottoman, or a chesterfield,
or a davenport, or so I expect.

The muse dips in her handbag,
and filches some silver.
She leaves
the waiter a quick, improbable tip.

III
The Muse and Her Moons

The doorbell rings. The muse,
dishevelled, in her party tartan dressing-gown,
her hair slurred,
sleepwalks to the door.

There is a shadow, haggling its hands,
at the step. It is the postman.
I bring you five moons, he announces,
scratching his forelock.
Special delivery.
He offers his regulation biro,
leaking, and requires
her signature's pigment.

Five moons. She signs,
sighs, slams the latch, and stands
in the archway, bemused.
What is this with moons?
She has not made him a moon
in a blue month of Mondays.

A thought strikes like a stone.
Wait! she calls, as his shadow
dissolves. *Yes, madam,* he says, a grin
foxing his face.
Take these moons, she tells him,
Remove them.

The postman traipses away,
with a bag of cracked moons, which he leaves,
unpublished, under
a bundle of bags and satchels.

1V
The Poet's Post

It's 8 a.m. The light knocks
softly at the letter-box; the mat
bristles with anticipation.

And then the sound of the feet
in the next street,
dodging the confluence of puddles.

The poet has sent
well-edited postcards to agents,
publishers, librarians, bookbinders,

and a get-well greeting
to a woman he once saw browsing
mind, body and spirit

in Waterstone's one Friday afternoon,
licking her lips and
footling some loose change.

Now he kneels by the door
waiting for
a rattle of replies. There is

a surreptitious click. The postman
pushes a single shaft
of light through the door.

It falls to the floor.
It is an invitation from a muse,
mirror-written, requesting

a meeting through a third party,
post-dated, and franked
the year before the year before last.

V

Going to Work

An alarm clock chucks me under the chintz
coverlet. I roll
over and over myself, and reach out
like a squid, to smack the snooze on: its colon
wibbles between 9 and 05. It is

another day, if you say so. The stilted
tick of the shutters, just ajar,
irritates me into opening
my wild green eyes. Yes, I'm a

muse. I am the one to whom you turn,
for instant alchemy, for the brainwave,
for the eye of an idea,
for the kick of an image, and just
possibly, a
publisher too. Oh

God, this is easy. Yes, dear. Obey
the genius within. That will be
fifty winks.

VI
Credit Where …

Brandy and ginger,
thank you.

I have provided you with five lines,
two words, three retractions,
and a semi-colon;
as yet, I have received no credit.

Bob is not my uncle, mate.
This is stiff work, a business,
I work from home at
uncharitable hours. In the morning,
usually in the morning, I sit
at my *tabula rasa*, and dandle
your memories. Or knit.

I have builders' bills, butcher's notes,
and a baker to pay. The florist alone
costs me a fortune.

As yet, I have had not even
a simple acknowledgement, not even
your dedication. It was
a gentleman's agreement.
A muse, after all, is a lady.
Here is the piano tuner, he is not blind,
that is a stereotype, he can see
I am undervalued.

I am going out for a walk
to throw my gauze gaze round the hills.
When I return, I trust
you will have settled the matter.
I do not believe in plastic.
Cash. Or a personal cheque
(in which case, in your best italic).
No loops. You may not
pay me in ribbon.

VII
Unwanted Visitors

The doorbell bawls. Fetching expletives
from a box by the back door, the muse
prepares to repel boarders.

I've warned you, she rehearses,
under her gleaming teeth and tongue.

At the door, she finds Mata Hari,
Scheherazade, Nefertiti, Delilah (why?),
Cruella De Vil, and – worst of all –
the bleeding Queen Of Sheba.
They have brought some scones.

We heard, they say, *that you have*
psychic power. We wondered if, perhaps,
over a glass of rhubarb, you would care to
address us on the subject of –

Over their heads, she pours
absinthe, goose-grease, the blushful
Hippocrene (Asda own-brand), Tizer,
and a dollop of
I Can't Believe It's Not Margarine.

Tarts! she says,
walloping the door, and
settling back to an
evening of
Ars Poetica.

VIII
The Blues

Her head is soup when he writes
a wriggle of questions
on pale blue foolscap, sent
by second class post.

He's vague, like a starfish
asking directions to the coastguard,
who wears a navy greatcoat,
and swivels his cobalt eyes.

Blues? she asks,
lifting her basking arm from a swathe of sofa,
do you mean
the painful refrains of impossible
old men who busked
in chain gangs, and scratched their voices
on shellac?

But he doesn't. Unable to complete
a line, he is looking for synonyms
like a glass eel hunting its colour.

Lupin, indigo, cyan, she tries;
woad. Cornflower, gentian,
the unmentionable blue of the bilberry,
the very vivid livid,
the blue of the blood spooling
beneath the skin. Marine. Or teal.
Arsenal away. The sailor
with his hopskip and jig. And jazz.

Will this do? She irritates her lips,
and franks his message with angry teeth.
That evening, she sleeps like an ocean.

IX
A Classic

She cracks open the pages,
which rustle with thumbs, and dives in
headfirst. The chapters are warm,
like lagoons well-swum.

She loves the splash
of the chapters, the way their
Roman numerals extend
from I to XXVII, the way
the binding invites her.

Her white arms
glide through the shallows,
and wrestle with the depths, all
latinate, lovely, pepped up with epigraphs.

Why, she wonders,
as the currents, flustered,
drag her through seas of greedy narrative,
does nobody ever
ask her
for inspiration like this? Why

has she been handed the grim
graft of the unwritten, unfinished, and somehow
ceaseless drivel of a badly-patched poet?
Who was the muse who
helped these wild tides rip? She faxes
her agent, raging. And plunges.

X
Coming Out

Leaning against marble, with her agent
counting her cut, the muse wears footwear
by Ferragamo. A jaunty halo
hovers above her, and her mouth moves
as if playing a solid silver flute.

For fifteen years, she remarks, *I have*
built up my bushel. Now it is time to set
fire to it. The flashlights
pander to her, magnesium moths
exploding, the ack-ack of paparazzi fracturing
the air (which pops with a chorus of corks).

Her collections fly off the shelves
like turtle doves. Her audiences form
orchestras and her name
brazens the billboards in capital cities.
She appears on Richard and Judy.
Who inspired you? he asks, elbowing into
the conversation. *Why, I did,* she answers,
blowing confetti from her licked lips.

XI
In Extreme Old Age

No slap. She handles a Bugatti
as well as her chauffeur, who glues his gloves
to the wheel. The road
is more fragile now, it steals away
like a figment.

Her ivory fingers tinker
with the breeze, play braille with her thigh.
She feeds oceans with fish.
She spoons
manuka honey into her tea, turns
over the leaves and stirs
interpretations, which she sips
through rubied lips.

She has read the last rites a thousand times.
So dull. She is
having them revised by a team of crack
priests in a honeycomb
of amber cells. Her trees
hum with a hundred words, the best ones,

the ones she concealed
from the poet, whose old *pocus*
she remembers only as embers which warmed
a winter solstice.

She plans an anthology
of fruits, of diamonds, and tarty sonatas.
Over her shoulder, she throws
a gin sling. Lovebirds perch
in her sinuous hair, but she could not
care less.

Cinnamon Press:

Find out more about Cinnamon Press, including our submissions policy and competitions for writers, at www.cinnamonpress.com

Other titles from Cinnamon Press:

Perhaps – **The 1st Cinnamon Press anthology**

The best entries in the first Cinnamon Press first collection award brought together in a rich anthology.

Relic Environments – Estill Pollock's sumptuous ninth collection – a poetic masterpiece.

Forthcoming titles:

The Lie of the Land – An Anthology of Contemporary Poetry from Wales – a wealth of poetry from well known names as well as original new voices. In aid of the Meningitis Trust in Wales. (May 2006, Hay on Wye festival)

Sound of Mountain – **Bruce Ackerley**

A collection at once simple and densely packed. Poems to read and reread: beautiful, visceral, uncluttered. (June 2006)

How to Marry the Dead – **Francesca McMahon**'s poignant, darkly comic novel is the story of Sue, whose daughter dies for no reason. Witty & sharply observed. (June 2006)

Autumn 2006 – Winter 2007 a series of first collections from new Welsh voices **clare e. potter, John Tanner, christopher brooke & Marilyn Jenkins**.

Look out for other new titles in fiction, non fiction and poetry from Shanta Everington, Ann Drysdale, Jane McKie, Louisa Adjoa Parker, Susan Richardson…